DANIEL SWAROVSKI

OPERETTE bag and jewels
"Cosmos" collection, FW 2004/05
Enfilage of crystal pearls

DANIEL SWAROVSKI

A WORLD of beauty

under the direction of Markus Langes-Swarovski

Thames & Hudson

Crystal has captured the mood of our moment, and yet it is the timelessness of this material, its ability to transcend fashions and trends, to reflect the dreams and desires of each age, that has turned it into an essential ingredient of creative expression today. Its lightness and brilliance, its intriguing contradictions of clarity and mystery, fire and ice, ethereal and physical, and most of all its inherent optimism have sparked the imagination of artists, artisans, and designers, in all areas of creativity, from fashion and jewelry to sculpture, interiors, and architecture. Through crystal they are bringing an air of celebration and luxury, a spirit of generosity and abundance into our everyday lives.

More than a century ago, an inspired Bohemian craftsman, Daniel Swarovski I, had a vision for crystal, and for the new century. Through his drive for innovation, and his technical virtuosity, crystal, the material he loved, became a microcosm of hope and light, of purity, femininity, and modernity, a vibrant, versatile material that made dreams come true for women all over the world. The mission to take crystal forward, to use it as a creative expression of the moment, seems to be stronger today than ever.

For these reasons and more, this book about the Daniel Swarovski line, named for the founder of the Swarovski company, and created in homage to his vision, not only celebrates the 15th anniversary of the line, but also looks into the infinite depths and possibilities of cut crystal. It is a story about freedom and poetry, about dreams that take their place in the very real world of today.

We very much hope you will enjoy exploring our world of crystal creativity in this book.

We have chosen to give the book a focal rather than a chronological structure, so that you can open it at any chapter, at any time, dipping in and out at will.

We invite you to share with us the poetry and enchantment, and the spirit of crystal.

Markus Langes-Swarovski, Member of the Executive Board

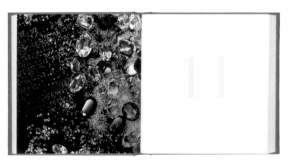

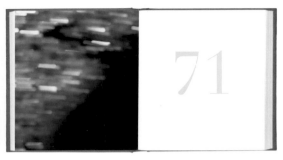

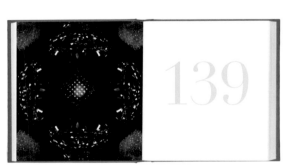

Inspirational *material*

Inspirational *material*

Inspirational material

Since 1989, the creations of Daniel Swarovski have told the tale of an extraordinary adventure revolving around the fascination of cut crystal. The adventure began some hundred years earlier, when Daniel Swarovski I (1862–1956) set up his own factory, installed with the first-ever machines for cutting and polishing crystal jewelry stones. Daniel Swarovski I devoted his technical prowess and his visionary talent to nurturing the poetic qualities of crystal, to revealing the beauty and soul of this material, its secrets and shadows, the dreams it promised and fulfilled.

From the moment the new, strong, lustrous lead crystal made its first appearance in the 18th century, the age of enlightenment, crystal has been regarded as a wondrous material, precious, aristocratic, desirable, with its own extraordinary qualities of brilliance, clarity, and majesty. Cut crystal has always possessed a unique capacity to capture and reflect light, enhancing and illuminating beauty.

The new 18th-century crystal could be cut and polished like gemstones, and in Paris, the royal jeweler, Strass, set foiled crystal gemstones into exquisite, exclusive jewels, adored by ladies of wealth and fashion.

Meanwhile, the Bohemian glass industry was flourishing, and by the mid-19th century it was celebrated for splendid *objets d'art*, prized by connoisseurs, and also for its world-leading speciality of expertly hand-cut crystal.

Immersed in this thriving industry, Daniel Swarovski I, a young Bohemian crystal-worker and budding scientist, visionary, and entrepreneur, was intent on perfecting both the material he worked, and the cutting techniques that unleashed its fire and light. Early on, as a teenager, painstakingly cutting crystal by hand in his father's workshop in a village near Gablonz, the center of Bohemian glass-cutting, Daniel Swarovski I became captivated by the positive, life-enhancing energy generated by this light-filled material. He understood the full potential of crystal, the freedom and fantasy it could bring to fashion and femininity, and set his mind to inventing the first machines for cutting and polishing crystal, and his heart on exploring the innate beauty of this material that had captured his imagination. Daniel Swarovski I was to give crystal a new dimension of luxury and dream-filled glamor, revealing its full potential as a creative, noble material.

A whole new chapter in the story of crystal was opened in 1895, when Daniel Swarovski I moved away from Bohemia, his homeland, to Wattens, a tiny, secluded village in Tyrol, Austria, to start a new life, and his own business, a factory producing mechanically cut and polished crystal jewelry stones. Wattens not only provided the necessary water power for the factory, but it was also conveniently situated on the train route to Paris, a route which also passed through Moscow, Prague, and Vienna.

The first Swarovski crystal stone, the famous *chaton*, a version of the classic brilliant cut, not only revolutionized the jewelry industry, but gave crystal an entirely new identity for the 20th century and beyond. The Swarovski *chatons*, precisely cut and faceted, and therefore more brilliant than before, also provided the industry with a new level of consistency, in terms of shape, size, facets, and luster. Swarovski's so-called *pierres taillées du Tyrol* glittered their way across the world on jewelry, hair ornaments, and shoe buckles, so that the company prospered and expanded. Later, in 1910, when Daniel Swarovski I set up a laboratory to manufacture his own raw material, he was able to refine and improve the crystal, aiming at a more intense and consistent brilliance. A little later still, he experimented with color, and from this starting point, with his beautiful, precision-cut, and sparkling material, Daniel Swarovski I ensured that crystal was linked to fashion, a vital ingredient in glamor, style, and the changing face of femininity.

DIAMANT bag
"Une soirée à l'Opéra" collection, SS 1991
Red lizard skin and cut crystal

Daniel Swarovsk I's mission was to ennoble crystal, to show crystal as a creative, versatile material in its own right, innovative rather than imitative. Yet at the same time he aimed to use crystal as a vehicle for sharing the joys of jewels, to introduce artistry and beauty to a wider, more democratic audience than ever before. It was a vital part of Daniel Swarovski I's vision to give women the freedom to express their personalities, their dreams and desires through jewelry they could buy for themselves.

NEPAL ring
"Riviera Rock" collection, SS 2004
Cut crystal

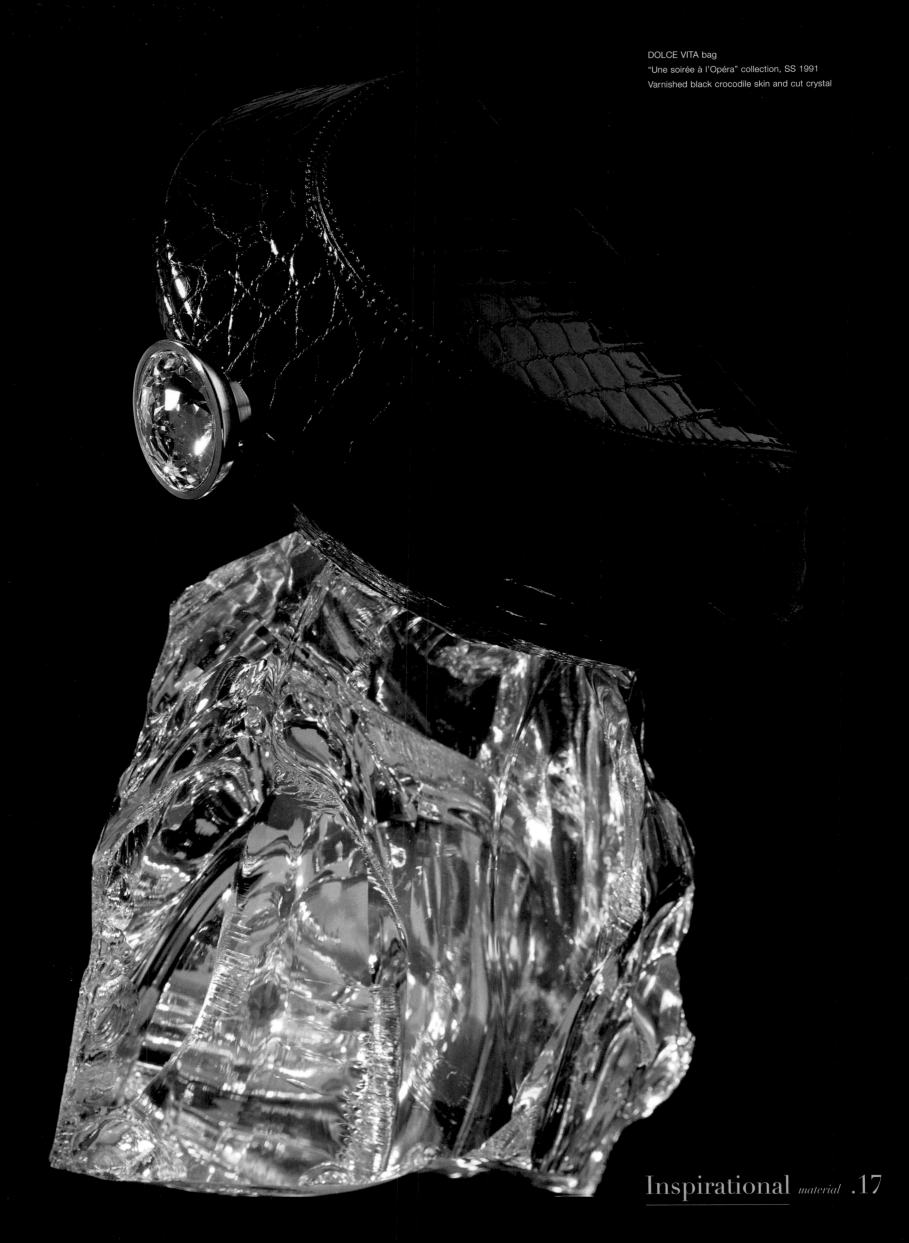

DOLCE VITA bag
"Une soirée à l'Opéra" collection, SS 1991
Varnished black crocodile skin and cut crystal

Inspirational *material* .17

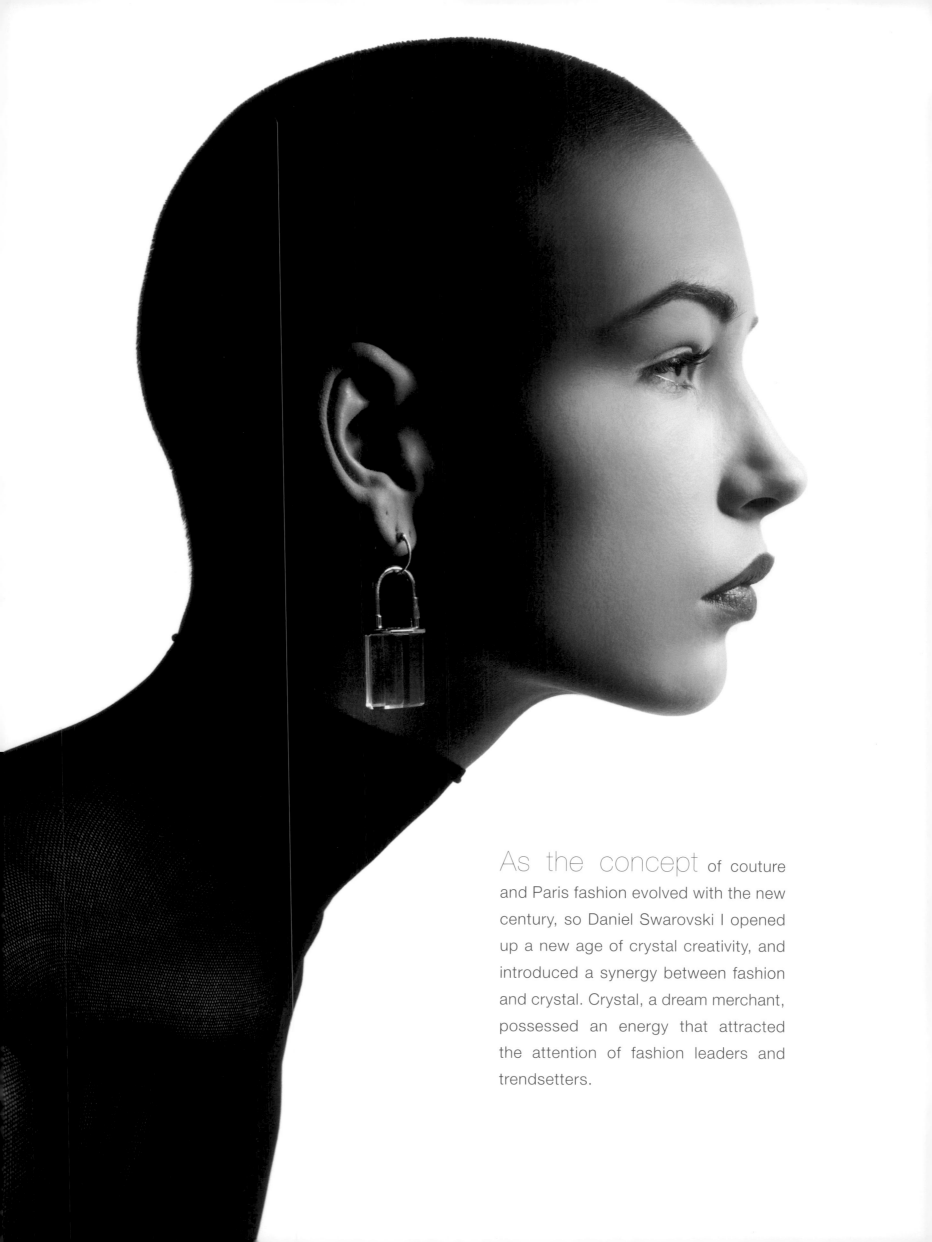

As the concept of couture and Paris fashion evolved with the new century, so Daniel Swarovski I opened up a new age of crystal creativity, and introduced a synergy between fashion and crystal. Crystal, a dream merchant, possessed an energy that attracted the attention of fashion leaders and trendsetters.

Daniel Swarovski I and his sons began to work closely with talented designers and their ateliers, with Chanel, Schiaparelli, and later Dior, adding opulence, extravagance, and Jazz Age pizazz, while Swarovski's own innate creativity and intense impulse toward innovation and ingenuity became a driving force within the fashion and jewelry industries.

HEMISPHERE bag
"Crystal Palace" collection, FW 1993/94
White satin and crystal pendants

Work

Inspiration and innovation. Behind the scenes, at Swarovski headquarters in Wattens, state-of-the-art technology and precision engineering join forces with timeless artistry and craftsmanship to conjure crystal into the stuff that dreams are made of. Sophisticated research and development laboratories, factories filled with high-tech cutting, coating, and polishing machines, invented and built by Swarovski, are fueled by an esthetic sensibility and a creative spirit that lie at the heart of the company.

shop
of dreams

Creative Director Rosemarie Le Gallais

Swarovski's technical virtuosity revolves around the company's passion for ideas, for invention and innovation, for continual experimentation, with all its trials, errors, and unexpected discoveries; a passion too, and respect, for the captivating qualities of crystal, the dreamlike, light-filled material itself, and most of all a passion for perfection and precision. Two worlds, two dimensions, two diametrically opposite attributes, poetic and scientific, instinctive and rational, the personal and the global, working together, to contrast and complement, in a dynamic dialogue of construction and creation.

Crystal, expertly precision-cut, colored, and immaculately finished to reveal its hidden depths, is transformed by artists and artisans into exquisite accessories, jewels, and design objects. Crystal dreams.

Workshop of dreams

The duality of technology and artistry, of science and poetry, that underpins Swarovski was handed down by the company's founder, Daniel Swarovski I. A technical prodigy and a visionary, an entrepreneur and a humanist, Daniel Swarovski I possessed a rare combination of talents. Apprenticed to his father, a crystal-cutter, in a remote mountain village in Bohemia, Daniel Swarovski I grew up to be an inventor, with a passion for mechanical ideas. He realized that new technologies, like electricity, could unleash the full potential of crystal, the material that fascinated and captivated him. At eighteen, he took his first invention, a machine for setting crystal stones, directly to Paris, the pulse of fashion and design, cementing the link between technology and artistry that has shaped the company ever since. Today, as always, the discipline of Swarovski's precision cutting and technical prowess provides artistic freedom. Technical expertise not only creates new crystal jewelry stones and textile applications, but also opens endless possibilities for breaking rules and boundaries, subverting conventions, for exploring crystal fantasies, bringing creative visions to life. In the small, intimate design ateliers of Daniel Swarovski in Paris, members of the creative team sketch, scribble, and play with the newest crystal stones and components, sent to them from Wattens. At other times, they dream up shapes, colors, textures, and forms, to express a particular theme, and to add to their crystal wish-list for forthcoming collections. They find the compelling duality of Swarovski's expertise reflected in the contrasts and contradictions of crystal itself, warm and cool, fire and ice, strong yet fragile, weighty yet ethereal, clear and secretive. Its poetic qualities set free by the ideas and mechanical inventions of Swarovski's extraordinary founder. The dream machines.

Daniel Swarovski I (1862–1956)

TE DEUM cross
SS 1997 collection
Cut crystal in a
hammered bronze chain
Cross initially conceived
for the church of Fritzens
(next to Wattens)

The original concept for the Daniel Swarovski collection aimed at reflecting the spirit of couture: jewels, handbags, and accessories, dedicated to beauty, thoughtfully conceived, exquisitely made from ravishing materials, impeccably cut and finished with sublime, handcrafted details, and always touched by an extravagant, indulgent fantasy, even eccentricity.

JAZZ necklace
"Crystal Palace" collection,
FW 1993 / 94
Enfilage of crystal pearls

LORELEI earrings and necklace
"Crystal Odyssey" collection,
SS 1994
Enfilage of crystal flowers

Couture
attitude

The Daniel Swarovski collection, alive with a dynamic interplay of themes and inspirations, an inventiveness and originality of form and function, reaches across categories and design disciplines, bringing jewelry, handbags, sunglasses, gloves, watches, body ornaments, fashion, and design objects together in a spirit of couture, fantasy, and refinement.

POLO Bag.JPG

POLO Bag.JPG

The essence of couture is expressed in the strong design ethos of Daniel Swarovski, as well as in its inventive and abundant use of crystal, and the ways in which designs emphasize the preciousness of the materials, incorporating bespoke crystal stones, like the oversized gems, specially developed and cut in Wattens exclusively for Daniel Swarovski. The spirit of couture lives too in the daring blend of crystal with unexpected materials, fur, feathers, lacquer, Plexiglas, semiprecious gems, and in intriguing handcrafted techniques. Each collection becomes a master performance, pushing crystal to new heights of fantasy and freedom.

The fluidity and flexibility that has become the signature of Daniel Swarovski's style provides a crucial link to the essential femininity of couture. Making crystal soft, deliquescent, full of light-catching movement, body-conscious sensuality, has been a mission, almost an obsession, at Daniel Swarovski. Crystal that flows, drapes, and folds, crystal turned into tactile, luxurious fabrics, mesh, macramé, chain mail, crystal with a hazy, soft, satin-like bloom, all redolent of the preciousness, ingenuity, and luxury of couture.

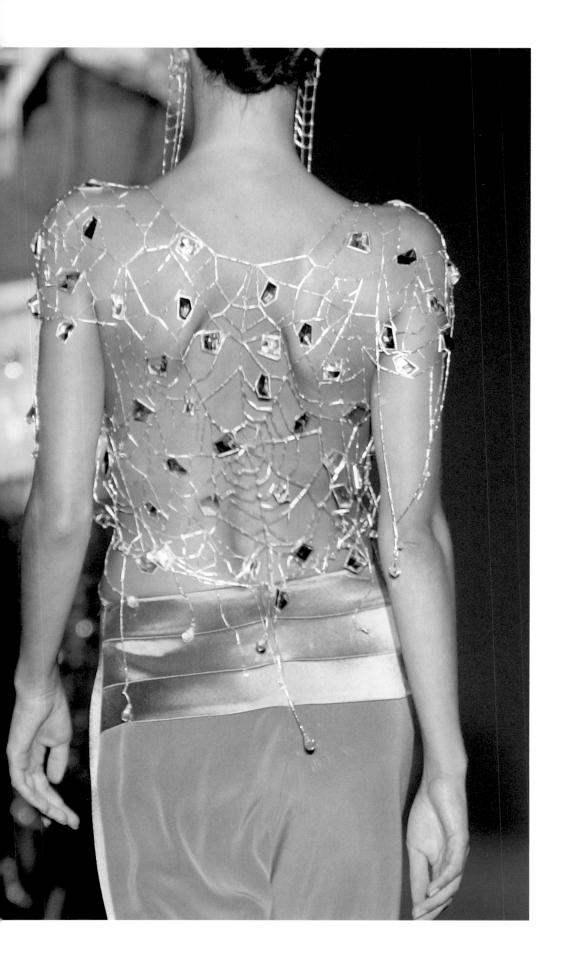

From the company's earliest days, from the beginnings of couture in the early 20th century, Swarovski has always worked hand in hand with the greatest designers, listening to their ideas and inspirations, translating their visions, developing a synergy which has resulted in crystal today becoming one of the most precious and expressive ingredients of fashion.

While Daniel Swarovski accessories capture the mood of the moment, *l'air du temps*, they are at the same time, like couture, beyond fashion; they represent a particular way of life, a philosophy, an attitude. At the core of this philosophy is a total dedication to femininity and perfection. Daniel Swarovski accessories have become a way of giving a woman the ease, confidence, and freedom to be herself, or become whoever she dreams of being. They reach out to women searching to unlock, in themselves, the individuality and creative courage that Daniel Swarovski represents.

COBWEB top
"Runway Rocks", Barcelona Gaudí Fashion Week, 2004
Network with asymmetrical cut-crystal stones

L'OFFICIEL

HARPER'S

Modèles exclusifs
Reproduction interdite

Jacques Heim. Cette robe en Cigaline Nylfrance de Bucol, couleur lavande, est de fines broderies du ton. Toute droite,
souple, elle s'orne de ... manches. Coiffure de Charles of the Ritz. Bijoux de Roger Jean-Pierre, en pierres taillées du Tyrol.
Christian Dior. Ravissante dans sa grâce délicate, cette robe de jeune fille est en Lorganza blanc de Bianchini-Férier. Une ganse de
satin vert émeraude souligne l'ourlet, l'encolure et le bas des manches évasées en forme de pagode, selon le thème de la collection.

True to oneself.

Daniel Swarovski takes its place in today's world of luxury as the couture signature of the Swarovski company, of its spirit of artistry, invention, and craftsmanship. It is a position that has been made possible by the company's expertise and experience in developing the art of crystal, and by its vital links to the worlds of jewelry, fashion, and couture that have grown organically and strengthened through the years. The full creative potential behind the vision could only have been unlocked by Swarovski's particular blend of technical prowess and manufacturing capabilities with the artisan-craftsman's sensitivities and passion for perfection. Swarovski gave form to Daniel Swarovski's visions through its expertise in cutting, faceting, polishing, and finishing crystal, and turned crystal into a living luxury through its love, respect, and understanding of the material. For centuries, the clarity and purity of crystal has symbolized truth: today, the Daniel Swarovski collection remains true to the company's core values of constant innovation and creativity, of openness and respect for the industries in which it is immersed, and respect for the world around it. Above all, Daniel Swarovski remains true to its founder's vision, linking past, present, and future in a progressive concept, aimed at a total design for living with crystal.

True *to on*

The creative dynamism that drives Swarovski as a company is powered by an inbuilt dedication to constant exploration and innovation, in both design and technology. A firm belief in continual progress, in improving and perfecting what has gone before, however good, has been an integral part of the company's philosophy since Daniel Swarovski I set up his pioneering crystal cutting factory in Wattens, Austria, in 1895.

.Continual
anticipation

ALASKA bag
SS 1998 collection
Black satin and crystal mosaic

The laboratory built in 1910 to produce and perfect the raw material enabled Daniel Swarovski I and his sons to manufacture their own superior, brilliant crystal, making the company independent and self-sufficient. It was a major step forward, leading to a vast palette of colors, cuts, and shapes, and, later, a series of spectacular coatings. The celebrated Aurora Borealis crystal stone, iridescent and shot through with fiery, rainbow glints, was created in the 1950s by Manfred Swarovski, the grandson of Daniel Swarovski I, especially for Christian Dior. The couturier's inspiration was drawn from the 18th-century magnificence of the candlelit mirrors and chandeliers of Versailles. The Aurora Borealis crystal bead became a worldwide phenomenon, its coating technique adapted through the years to produce other Swarovski classics such as hematite or the matt satin-effect jewelry stone.

Today's Daniel Swarovski team is immersed in this tradition of endless experimentation and innovation. Working closely with Wattens, in a synergy that marries creativity and technology, Daniel Swarovski has masterminded new techniques and creative effects that take crystal into a new dimension. At the same time, their challenging demands generate new product ideas for Wattens, unexpected shapes and textures for crystal stones, the monumentally oversized jewelry stones, and the irregular, asymmetric cuts, opaque, ceramic-like matt surfaces, a mirrored, metallic gleam.

Detail of LIMELIGHT bag
"Mirage" collection, SS 2003
Black satin with embroidery of
crystal stones and fine stones

From the very first collections, Daniel Swarovski has pioneered an exquisite technique of bejeweled crystal hand-embroidery, mixing crystal of different shapes and textures with gold thread or gemstones, creating pictorial effects, 18th-century-style *trompe-l'œil* motifs, or contemporary abstract designs, always soft and sumptuous, and linking crystal very firmly to the art of couture.

METAMORPHOSE bag
"Crystal Rhapsody" collection, FW 1994/95
Black satin embroidered and hand-painted
with crystal flakes

IN TIME bag
"Crystal Palace" collection, FW 1993 / 94
Pocket-watch bag embroidered with
gold thread and crystal

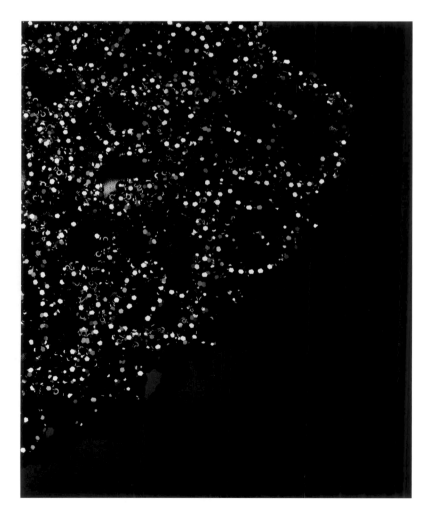

The mission to make crystal as soft and fluid as silk gave birth to various techniques of knitting, threading, or crocheting crystal into a supple, macramé-like crystal yarn. The technique known as *enfilage* is a cross-breed of several different traditional handicrafts, blended to produce something entirely modern yet with echoes of the past, transforming crystal into a supple, feminine, haute-couture version of chain mail.

Detail of GLORIA bag
"Polychrome" collection, SS 2001
Crystal Mesh pattern, multi comet and light silver

In the first few years of the Daniel Swarovski collection, Creative Director Rosemarie Le Gallais had dreamt of being able to turn crystal into a material, a crystal fabric that draped around the body, falling in fluid folds, like cascades of light. As Crystal Mesh was being invented in Wattens, so the Daniel Swarovski team were devising ways of working with this sensually flexible crystal fabric, using it on handbags and bracelets, creating patterns, stripes, graphics, flowers, animal-skin prints, and more. Crystal Mesh, continually changing, evolved into Crystal Tweed, a classic, couture-inspired pattern, and also into Pearl Mesh with its soft, secretive sheen.

Pearl Mesh was the result of a collaboration between the technical virtuosity of the teams in Wattens and the vision of Rosemarie Le Gallais, who had always loved the soft sheen of velvet. The new pearlized mesh that was born from this collaborative teamwork, composed of smooth, unfaceted crystal cabochons, was first shown to the world in the Daniel Swarovski collections.

Crystal Pearl Mesh
Crystal material with
silk-velvet effect

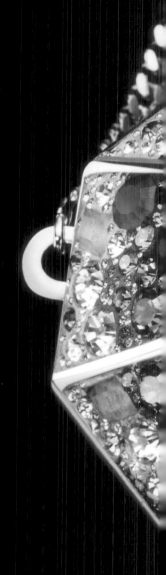

OURSIN ring
"Cosmos" collection, FW 2004/05
Crystal mosaics

Sculptural, heavily encrusted, uneven mosaic work on early Daniel Swarovski handbags led the way forward for a continually evolving range of jewels and accessories using a richly encrusted crystal *pavé* effect. The classic *pavé* technique, using a special adhesive developed by Swarovski, is made modern and organic by the random arrangement of differently sized and shaped crystal stones, creating a sumptuous texture with movement, shadow, and depth.

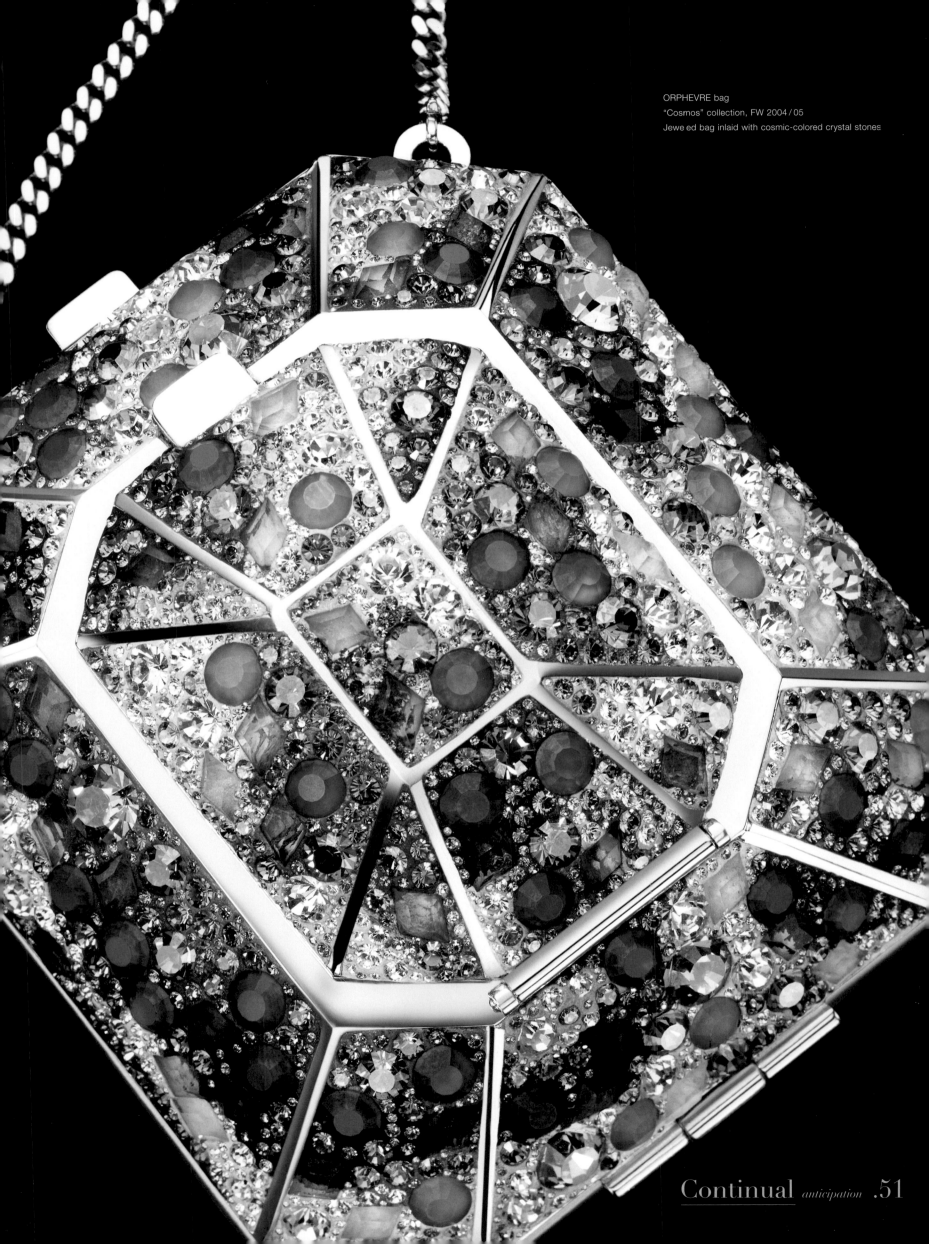

ORPHEVRE bag
"Cosmos" collection, FW 2004 / 05
Jewe ed bag inlaid with cosmic-colored crystal stones

Continual *anticipation* .51

Chatonnage, Daniel Swarovski's profusion of bezel-set stones, is adapted from a fine jewelry technique, especially used for diamonds, in which claw-set gems, clustered in random arrangements, are made to look as if they are light, weightless, free-floating, with little or no visible means of support. Daniel Swarovski, making the most of the freedom and fantasy of crystal, takes the technique to its extreme, hand-setting lively groups of massive crystal stones in abundance, creating a rhythmic composition of size and shape, playing with contrasts of the gems and the empty spaces between them.

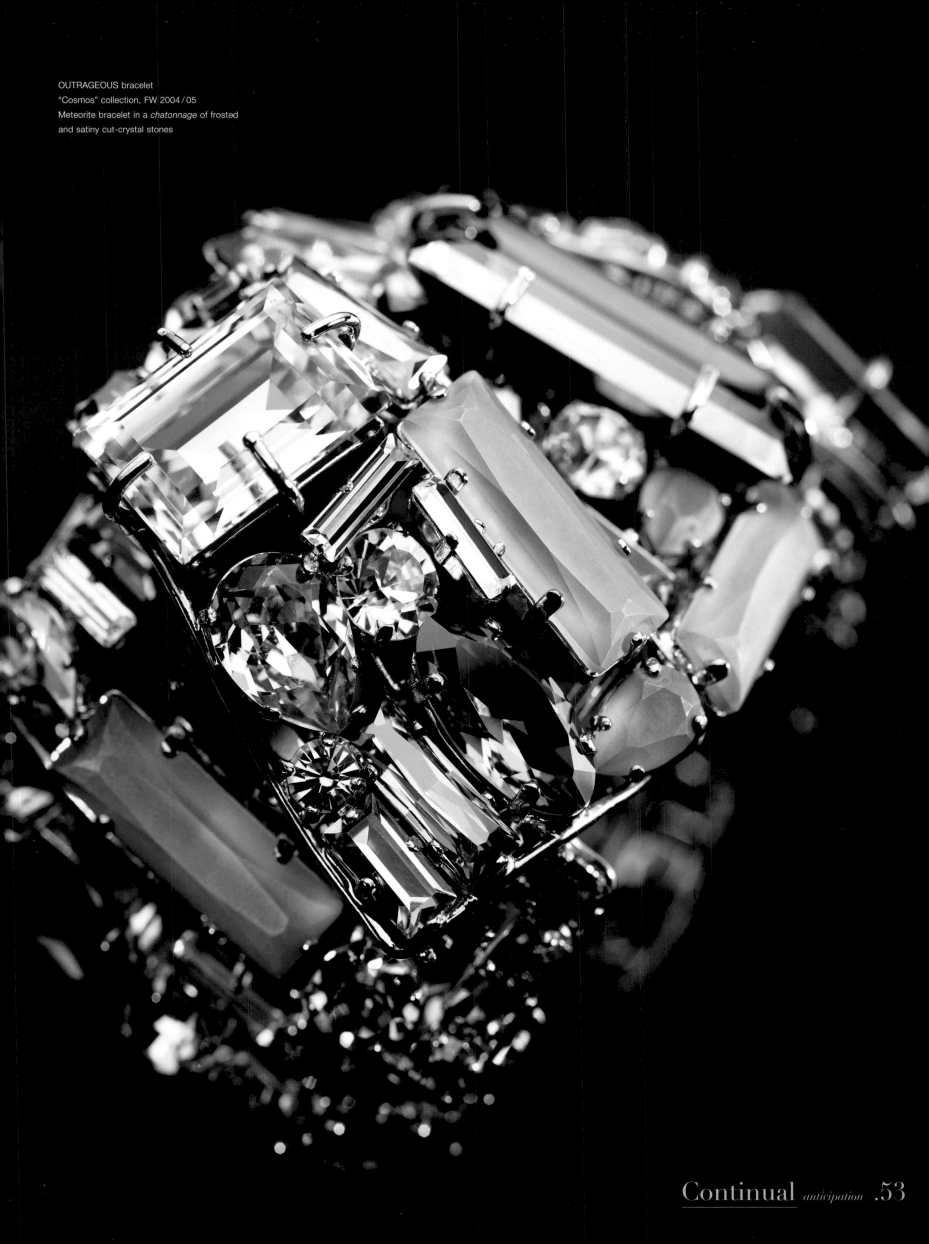

OUTRAGEOUS bracelet
"Cosmos" collection, FW 2004 / 05
Meteorite bracelet in a *chatonnage* of frosted
and satiny cut-crystal stones

HERMINE necklace
"Nouvel âge de bronze" collection, FW 2001 / 02
Jewels with a fur effect in gold and hematite
crystal stones

Crystal Fur is the evocative name given to Daniel Swarovski's special way of using crystals heavily clustered onto chain mail, with an effect that resembles the deep, tactile texture of fur, which can be stroked in one direction or another. Crystal Fur took the concept of Crystal Mesh in a more heavily bejeweled direction: a crystal fabric, equally tactile and fluid, yet encrusted with a lush thickness of densely packed dangling crystal stones that move on different planes. Once the idea had taken hold, Daniel Swarovski in Paris worked closely with Wattens to develop a special metal chain-mail base, with the right crystal stones and settings to achieve the desired effect. A metallic coating added a modern, mysterious look. and long, slender *navette*-cut stones contributed to the dreamy effect of deep, soft, crystal fur.

Daniel Swarovsk's urge to push limits and visions of crystal artistry and technology ripples outward into the company's design-led initiatives, like Crystal Palace and Runway Rocks, both aimed at attracting the world's cutting-edge creators to come up with new visions for crystal. For Crystal Palace, Swarovski invites international designers to reinvent the chandelier, for today, and for the future, in their own individual styles, encouraging them to give free rein to their imagination, with no commercial constraints. Runway Rocks challenges jewelry and fashion designers from around the world to come up with their own vision of jewelry for the catwalk, pushing boundaries of form and meaning, highlighting the often "invisible" art of the catwalk jewel. So the thrill goes on, the fevered search for an as-yet undiscovered crystal sensation, the expectation of new crystal creativity, endless crystal reflections.

Detail of MISIA bag
"Vie sauvage" collection, FW 2003 / 04
Enfilage and *chatonnage* of matt multicolored crystal stones

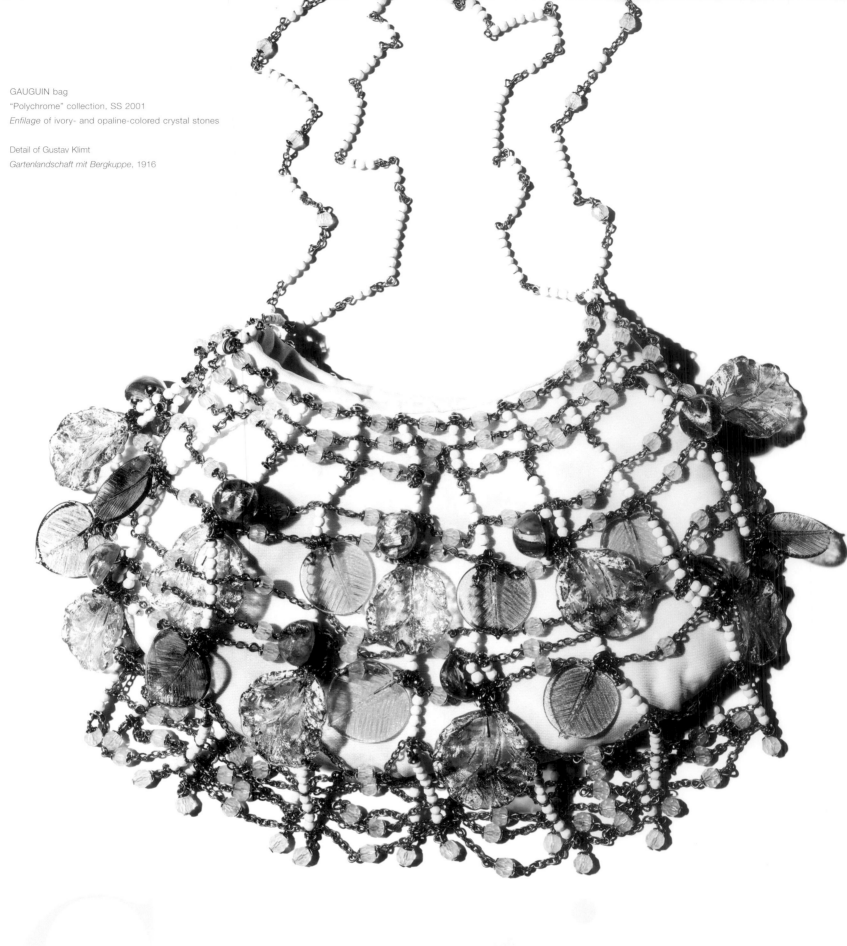

GAUGUIN bag
"Polychrome" collection, SS 2001
Enfilage of ivory- and opaline-colored crystal stones

Detail of Gustav Klimt
Gartenlandschaft mit Bergkuppe, 1916

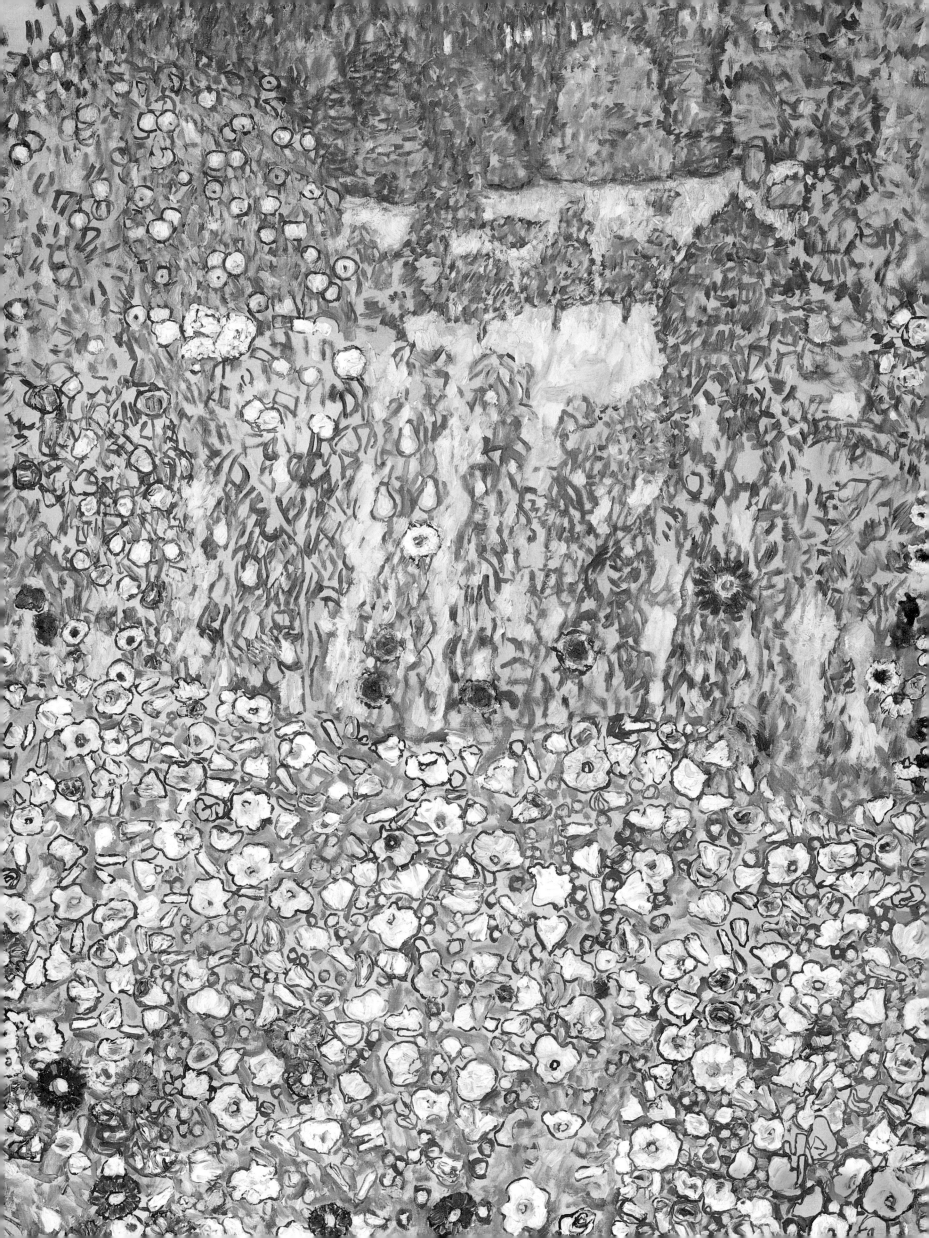

Creative origins

Daniel Swarovski's creative team taps into a rich source of ideas and inspirations, iconography drawn from the widest possible spectrum of themes, from ethnic art and tribal jewelry, a perennial, universal inspiration, raw and earthy, to contemporary art and iconic 20th-century jewels, intellectual and sophisticated. The fast-moving series of cultural and historical scenarios forms a backdrop to Daniel Swarovski's own innovative creativity, so that themes serve only as veiled inspirations, translated freely into Daniel Swarovski's distinctive visual language.

But from the midst of this overflowing source of inspiration springs Swarovski's own rich and resonant cultural heritage. The company's roots, first in Bohemia in the late 19th century and then in Austria at the dawn of the new century, reach back into turn-of-the-century *Mitteleuropa*, digging deep into the last frenetic, pleasure-filled years of the magnificent, multicultural Austro-Hungarian Empire. Between them, the flamboyant cities of central Europe, Prague, Budapest, Bucharest, Vienna, brewed an intoxicating mix of art, music, literature, science, intellectual brilliance, a ferment of East and West. This was the radiant world of Strauss and Rilke, Klimt and Liszt, of Freud and Einstein. An enchanted world filled with the waltz and the operetta, cafés and pleasure gardens, with gypsies and dashing uniformed officers, Turkish pashas and Balkan princes, its intense frivolity and sensual overload rocked by an undercurrent of nostalgia and malaise. This extraordinary cultural melting-pot, at the heart of Europe, at the start of a new century, sent waves around the world.

Vienna, where the young Daniel Swarovski I visited the first International Electric Exhibition in 1883, and where he worked for a while some years later, was a vibrant *Belle Epoque* city, the City of Dreams, alive with baroque beauty, style, fashion, high society, music and above all, with the cult of femininity, so poignantly portrayed by Gustav Klimt. Some of the most beautiful and stylish women in Europe rode their carriages in the Prater, Vienna's famous park, drank coffee at Sacher, listened to poetry readings at the famous cabaret club Die Fledermaus, waltzed endlessly through the many masked balls of the annual Carnival. Yet, at the same time, a serious-minded, progressive thread of art, architecture, and design emerged from the melee, heading toward modernism, and the new democratic concept of integrating art into every aspect of daily life, making good design available to all. The idealistically based arts and crafts workshop, the Wiener Werkstätte, established in 1903 by Josef Hoffmann and Koloman Moser to revitalize the decorative arts, championed hand-workmanship, the marriage of form and function, and the human touch.

CRYSTAL OBJECT 2
FW 1989/90 collection
Alessandro Mendini
Cut crystal

MAYERLING gloves
FW 1989/90 collection
Fan-cuff black suede with
crystal motif embroidery in the
Viennese Secession style

HANS bag
FW 1989/90 collection
Black suede with crystal
mosaic embroidery

The Wiener Werkstätte's architectural, geometric, and stylized organic designs, its black-and-white color schemes, its dedication to design, craftsmanship, and humanity helped shape the first-ever Daniel Swarovski collection. A collection, sharp, chic, and forward-looking, paying homage to a past world in which the company's founder was immersed.

Gustav Klimt
Die Erfüllung, 1905–9

JAPAN necklace
"Tribal Attraction" collection, SS 2000
Tie-shaped necklace, *enfilage* of leather,
crystal, and ivory resin

MARLY necklace
"Vie sauvage" collection, FW 2003/04
Composition of crystal stones and
fawn-colored pheasant feathers

PATCHWORK cuff bracelet
"South Pacific" collection, SS 2005
Tropical-colored graffiti paving

Contemporary art adds another ingredient to Daniel Swarovski's melting-pot of themes and inspirations. 20th-century paintings, including works by Kandinsky and the Russian Expressionists, with their dynamism, mix of colors, broken lines, planes, and graphic statements, serve as a catalyst for Daniel Swarovski's designs. It is, explains Creative Director Rosemarie Le Gallais, a question of translating the emotional response to a painting, rather than the painting itself. "It is about observation, and interpreting the positive energy or the feeling a painting generates. The same painting can give different inspirations, depending on what you're searching for at the time. Then you have to find a way of bringing this inspiration or feeling into today's world of fashion and design."

Lines in motion. Filled with the pure energy of light, cut crystal is alive with a constantly moving play of light, an inner dynamism of lines, angles, and planes in perpetual movement, throwing luminous beams in different directions. Crystal beckons light with each movement of the body. Its radiance, shadow, and nuances of color seem to slide and shift as you look deep into the crystal from different angles. Swarovski crystal is composed of linear structures carefully plotted and planned to catch and refract the light. Precision-cut facets create the play of light and energy within the crystal, releasing its brilliance. They create optical effects, a visual game of interlocking lines, stimulating the imagination, suggesting limitless depths, blurring of boundaries, between light and shade, reality and fantasy. Crystal, pure poetry in motion.

The Metal

KYRAT pendant
"Mirage" collection, SS 2003
Drop of cut crystal set in solid silver

morphosis
of luxury

ORNEMENT bag
"Cosmos" collection, FW 2004 / 05
Powder-gold canvas and multi crystal

Daniel Swarovski brings luxury to a wider audience, and to a new individualistic audience, without sacrificing quality, creativity, or design excellence.

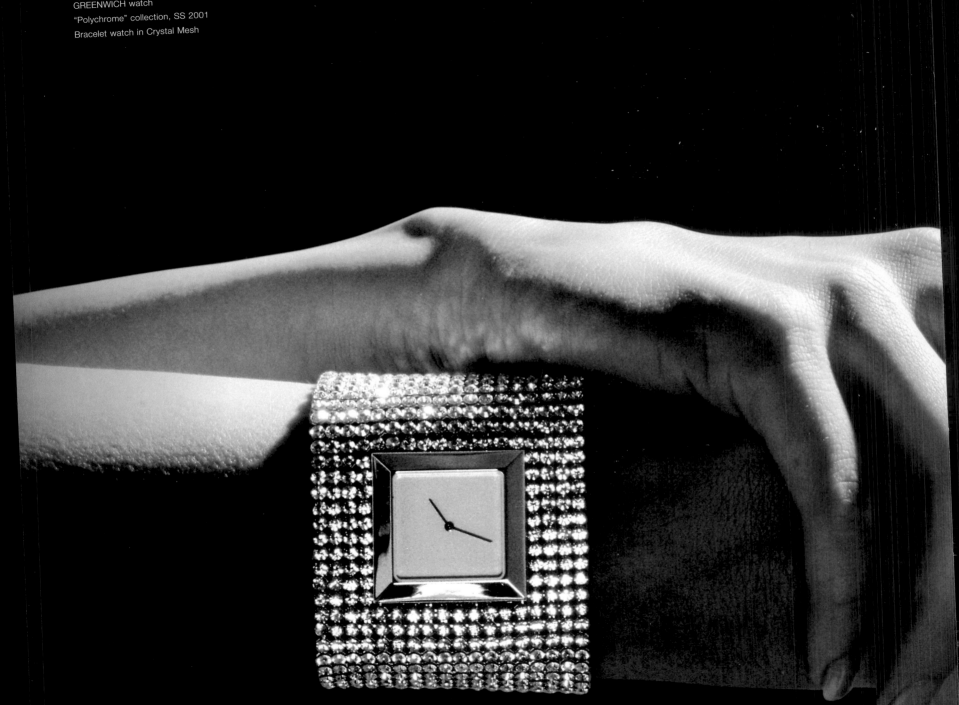

GREENWICH watch
"Polychrome" collection, SS 2001
Bracelet watch in Crystal Mesh

The Daniel Swarovski collection has given crystal a new lease of life, a new seductive appeal to the 21st-century woman. The role of crystal in luxury has changed, cutting across categories and design disciplines, from clothes and jewels to interiors and objects, injecting a positive attitude, poetry, and fantasy into accessories, which have become the most desirable and directional element of fashion. Daniel Swarovski crystal accessories are now worn for all occasions, even with sportswear and jeans, producing a provocative contrast of precious opulence with casual modernity.

RAY art object
Collection of designer objects, SS 2002
Darko Mladenovic
Block of cut crystal
Limited edition

KYRAT pendant
"Mirage" collection, SS 2003
Drop of cut crystal set in solid silver

NOE cross
"Mirage" collection, SS 2003
Cut crystal set in solid silver

Cuff bracelets
SS 1999 collection
Crystal Mesh

NUMBER ONE wristwatch
FW 2003 / 04 collection
Jewelry watch in white gold and
crystalline ingots in cubic zirconium
Fitted with a Swiss-made quartz movement
Limited series

When the Daniel Swarovski collection was first conceived in the late 1980s, minimalism ruled the style world, and jewelry and accessories had been largely banished from fashion, from women's lives. Yet Creative Director Rosemarie Le Gallais had a strong and clear vision for Daniel Swarovski, based on a metamorphosis of luxury, in which the roles of clothes and accessories would be reversed, clothes would become simpler, more comfortable, and accessories would take the starring role.

"Our lifestyles were becoming faster, women were traveling extensively," explains Rosemarie Le Gallais. "One of the best ways for a woman to be glamorous and individual in such a fast-paced existence is through accessories."

NEPAL ring
"Riviera Rock" collection, SS 2004
Cut crystal

CRYSTAL SQUARE spectacles
"Boutique" collection, 2003
Grey shades studded with two rows
of morion-colored crystals

The evolution of Daniel Swarovski reflects the vision of the company's founder. Daniel Swarovski I wanted to show the world the precious nobility of crystal, an endlessly versatile and expressive material with extraordinary qualities, yet also to make beautiful jewels available to all women, to enhance their lives and their beauty through crystal. As luxury today has grown into an entire universe built on dreams and associations, more focused on design, it has also become less elitist and more of a social leveler.

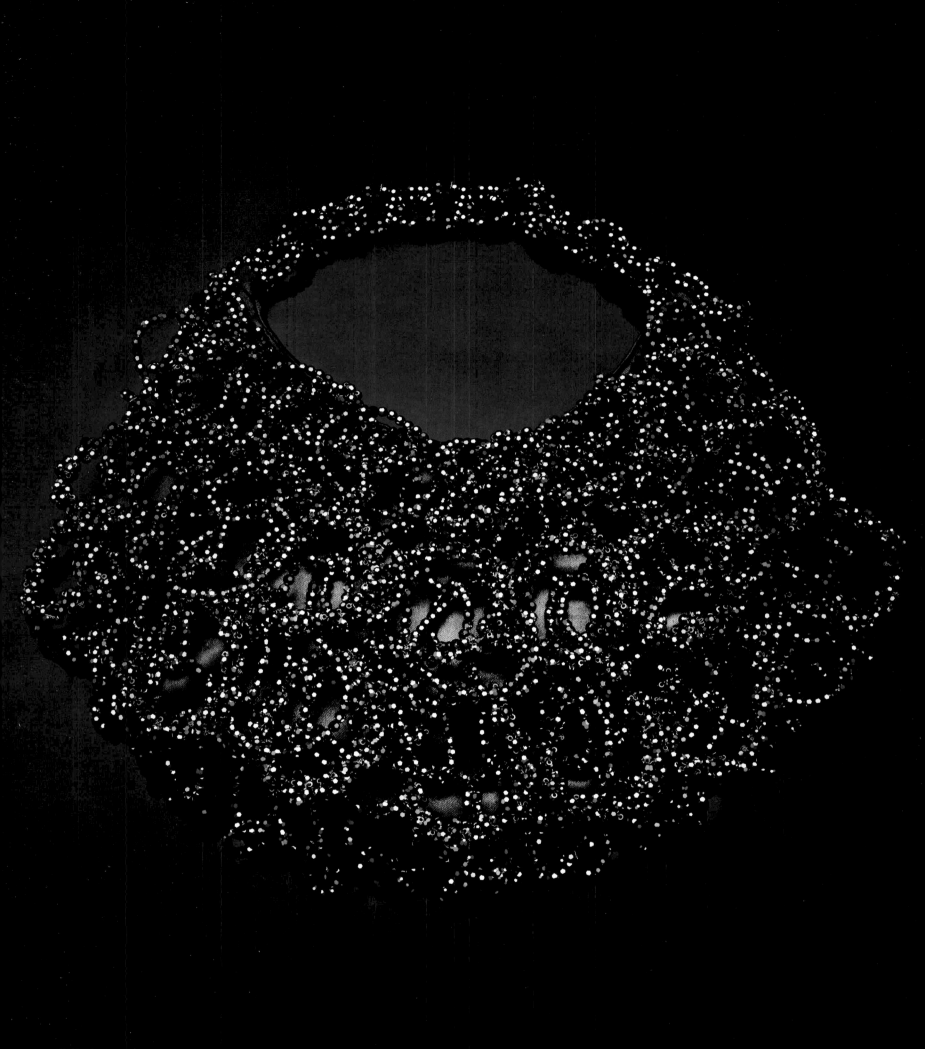

KRISTINA bag
"Sur la route de la soie" collection, FW 2002 / 03
Evening mesh with 10,000 hematite crystal pearls
Limited edition

OPHELIA bag
SS 1995 collection
Enfilage of jet-black and navy-blue crystal pearls

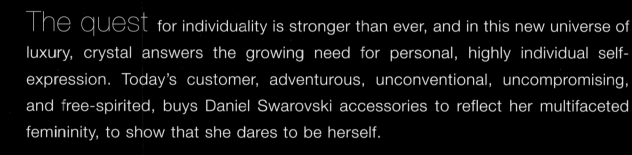

The quest for individuality is stronger than ever, and in this new universe of luxury, crystal answers the growing need for personal, highly individual self-expression. Today's customer, adventurous, unconventional, uncompromising, and free-spirited, buys Daniel Swarovski accessories to reflect her multifaceted femininity, to show that she dares to be herself.

The Metamorphosis *of luxury*

OH LA LA bag
SS 1995 collection
Enfilage of rosaline crystal stones

Filled with the light of inspiration and imagination, crafted with passion, crystal is touched with poetry and intimacy, enriching our world and our lives. There is poetry in its inner light, rhythmic, lyrical, that captures and reflects our dreams and desires. Mirror-like, crystal shows you your soul; its otherworldly qualities of clarity and purity have always symbolized truth. Lose yourself in its depths; find yourself in its memories and reflections. Swarovski crystal, with its fiery brilliance, resonates with enchantment and celebration, reinforcing us with positive energy.

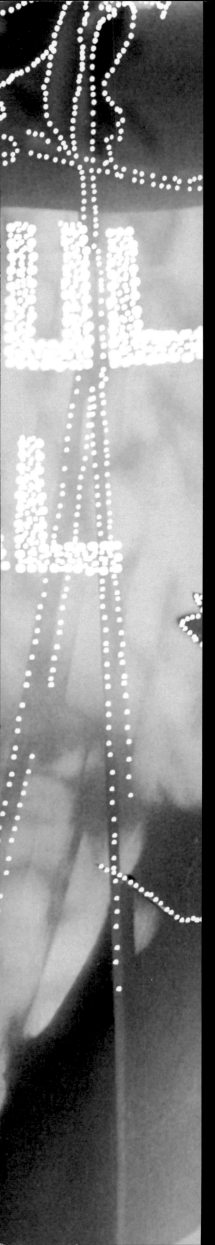

Jewelry, like poetry, is a way of interacting with the world, and Swarovski crystal reaches out with its own poetic language, poignant, powerful, moving, capable of expressing the widest range of emotions, profound or fleeting, joyful or haunting. It is a rich language that inspires and shapes the creation of the crystal object.

Crystal becomes a ferryman, carrying us back and forth between fantasy and reality, and like poetry, showing us new perspectives, new ways of understanding the world around us. Crystal, the material with a soul.

Detail of Daniele Buetti
Is the soul immortal?
Lightbox, 2004

ABSOLUT ZODIAC
Illustration of sign of the zodiac Pisces
for Absolut Vodka calendar, 1999
Crystal hat for romantic Piscean

Crystal
Glamor

Crystal embodies glamor, that indefinable, alluring branch of beauty. Its radiant light, its mix of strong style and irresistible magnetism have always given crystal an innate glamor, which has been explored by the Daniel Swarovski creative team. Swarovski crystal now, as ever, defines and highlights the changing femininity of each age, adding its own signature of style and glamor. Jewel-encrusted *Belle Epoque* beauties, along with cabaret stars like Mistinguette or Josephine Baker, and Hollywood idols from Marlene Dietrich to Marilyn Monroe, have always turned to crystal to emphasize their star quality.

NEPAL ring
"Riviera Rock" collection, SS 2004
Cut crystal

Crystal *glamor* .99

Crystal glamor

From its beginnings, cocooned in the elegance of the *Belle Epoque*, Swarovski has worked with the light-filled power of crystal. Around the turn of the century, lavish jewels, hair combs, and glinting shoe buckles were set with Swarovski's crystal jewelry stones, the celebrated *pierres taillées du Tyrol*. They added tantalizing touches of light, from head to toe, for the lady of fashion. Swarovski's new precision-cut *chatons* were more brilliant than any other crystal stones before them.

Expensive and considered a precious and exclusive luxury, they were very often mixed with precious metals, hand-set into desirable, fashionable jewels that were sold alongside fine jewelry. As these jewels exuded high-octane glamor, Swarovski crystal stepped forward into the spotlight of fashion and beauty.

NEPAL ring
"Riviera Rock" collection, SS 2004
Cut crystal

KIOSQUE bag
"Sur la route de la soie" collection, FW 2002 / 03
Crystal Mesh

PAPARAZZI spectacles
2004 collection
Midnight-black shades studded with
a web of transparent crystals
Limited edition of 10 pieces

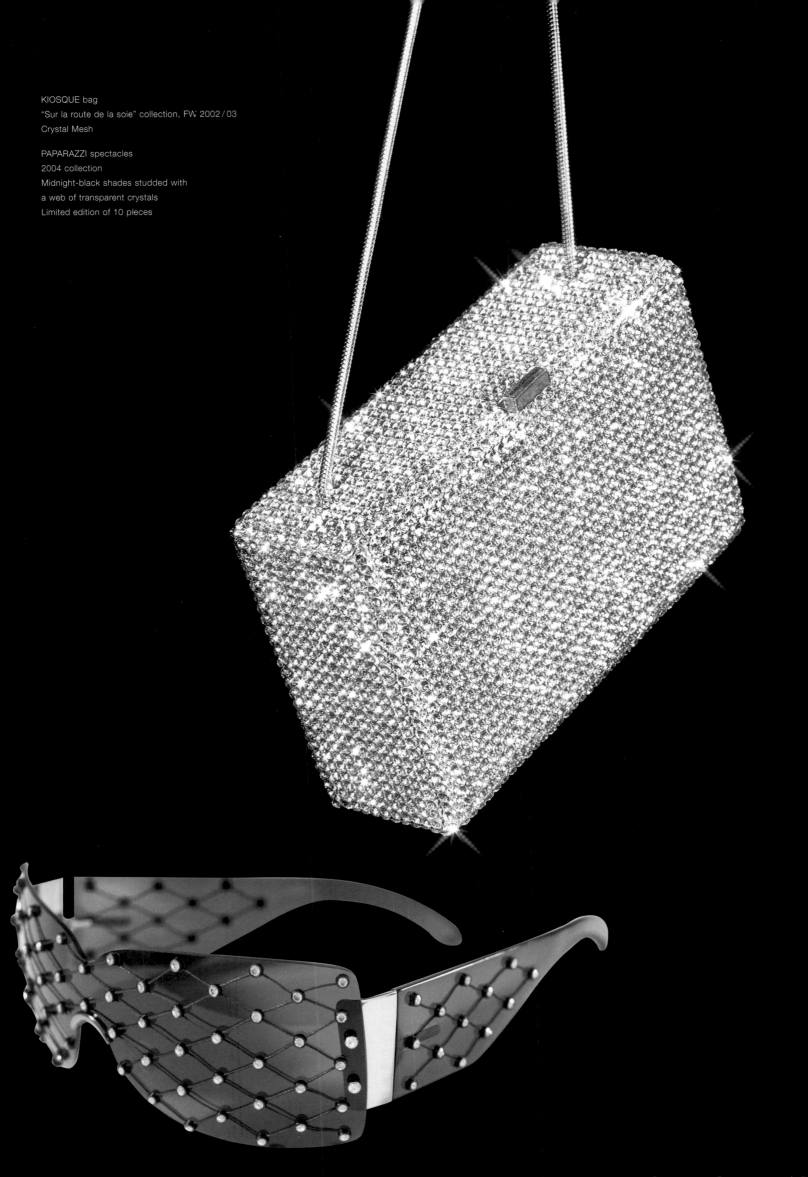

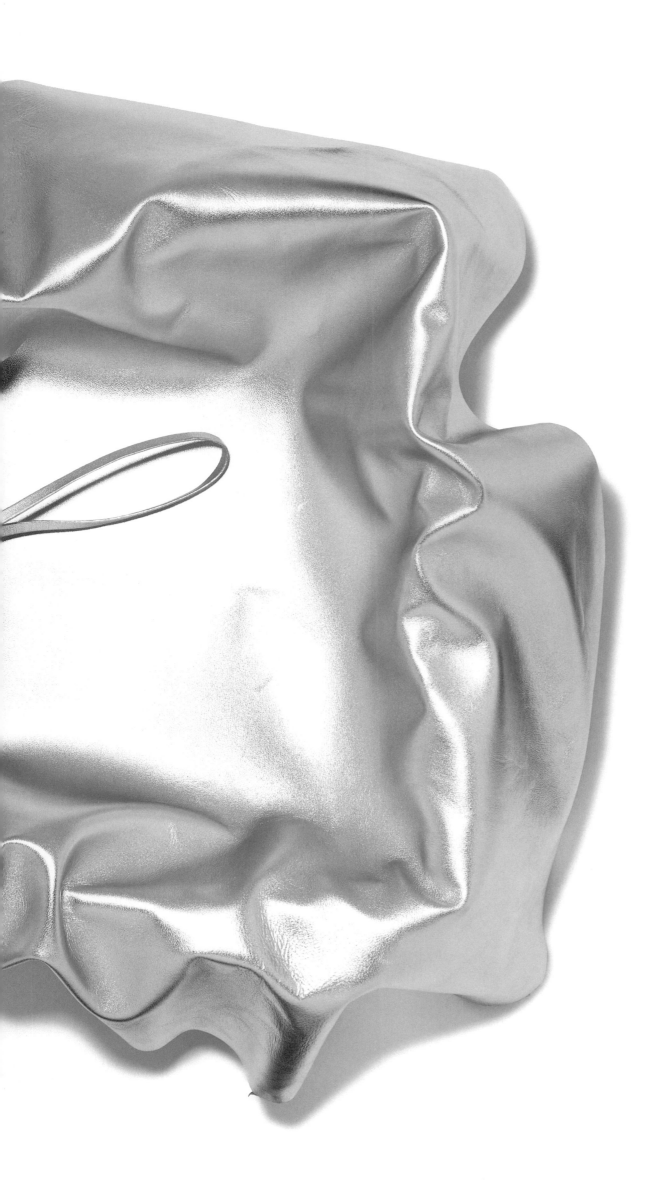

NEW YORK bag
"Riviera Rock" collection, SS 2004
Pale-gold lambskin inlaid with a jewel
of cut crystal stones

Crystal *glamor* .105

Once again, today Swarovski crystal takes center stage in the world of celebrity style. Daniel Swarovski's attention-loving jewels and handbags parade along the red carpets and flash in the spotlights of the world's most glamorous, star-studded events, celebrity parties, film premieres, the Cannes Film Festival, the Oscars. Crystal captures the limelight.

STAR COLLECTOR
bracelet jonc
SS 2004 collection
Crystal Mesh
Limited edition,
created for the 2004
Cannes Film Festival

MAGIE necklace
"Vie sauvage" collection, FW 2003 / 04
Enfilage of crystal stones

Creative *spirit*

A powerful impulse toward constant creativity, both artistic and technical, is the driving force behind Daniel Swarovski. Led by Creative Director Rosemarie Le Gallais, the creative team, based in Paris but with links to every fashion capital of the world, is ceaselessly searching for new ideas, inspirations, and innovations, driven to push the boundaries of form, function, and beauty. Their aim is to change the universal perception of cut crystal, to find new creative expressions for crystal by challenging conventions of color, form, and scale, translucencies and texture. At the same time, Daniel Swarovski breaks entrenched rules of jewelry-wearing, crossing borders, extending the whole concept of the jewel in our lifestyles today. So that a handbag becomes a precious, personal treasure, gem-shaped or crystal-encrusted, and a jewel becomes a body ornament, a fabric, or an item of clothing. It is, explains the team, a continuing, ongoing journey of exploration. The Daniel Swarovski collection is very much a work in progress. Creating crystal without frontiers.

Collage by Rosemarie Le Gallais

NADJA cuff bracelet
"Riviera Rock" collection, SS 2004
Chatonnage of crystal stones and turquoises

The creative process at Daniel Swarovski is intensely individual and spontaneous, following its own unpredictable path of freedom and fantasy. Crystal, the material itself, with its depths and secrets, its reflections and contradictions, provides the starting point for endless inspirations and interpretations.

"Inspiration comes from whatever you live through." For Rosemarie Le Gallais, creativity means spontaneity, responding to myriad stimuli in our world, all day, everyday. It may be a color, texture, or patina, a cloud, a waterfall, a mountain view in Wattens. A kaleidoscope of shifting visions, gathered together into a sophisticated, modern baroque style, eccentric and extravagant. A style in which glimpses of past, present, and future, of art and nature are layered with cultural references, visual games of contrast and contradiction, sensual surfaces of shine or shadow.

Collage by Rosemarie Le Gallais

The vitality of design is brought to life through the unrivaled craftsmanship of specialist artisans, sought out and nurtured by the Daniel Swarovski creative team. Recherché techniques are often cross-bred to create fresh technical virtuosity, in which crystal flirts with unexpected materials, feathers, fur, Plexiglas, leather, silk, shagreen, or plays with silver and natural gemstones. Daniel Swarovski's most famous innovations, blending artistry and artisanship, include sculptural mosaics, rich crystal embroideries, macramé or "knitted" crystal, encrusted crystal chain mail, all expressed in subtle or thrilling painterly combinations of color, shape, and texture.

JET bag
"Tribal Attraction" collection, SS 2000
White lambskin paved with crystal and
molten-glass cabochons

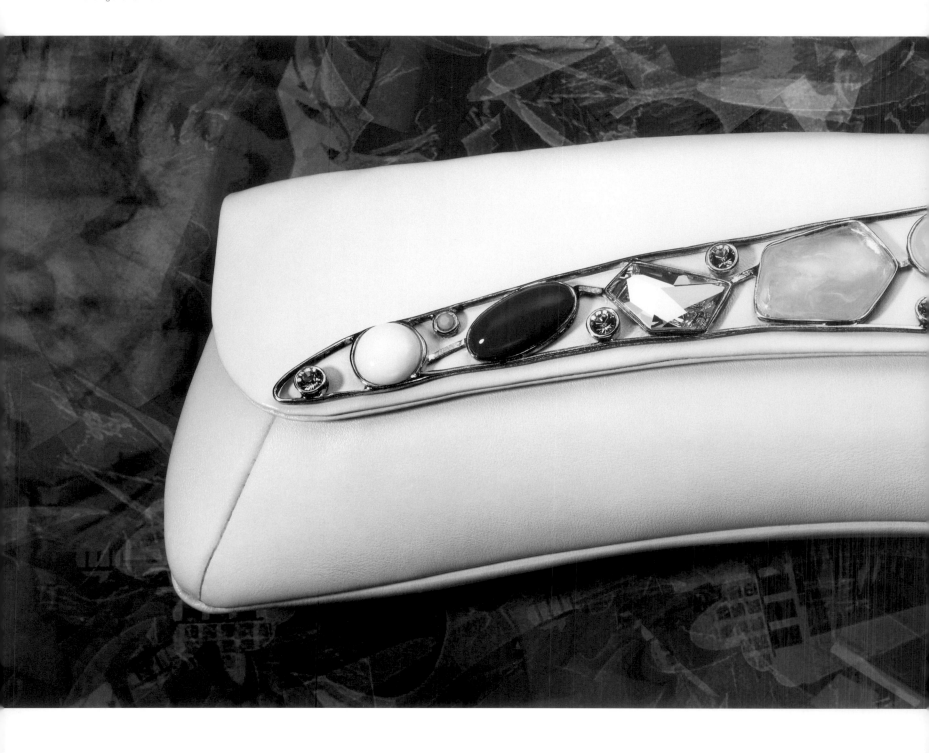

Collage by Rosemarie Le Gallais

Each Daniel Swarovski creation tells its own complex story of light and shadow, playful or soulful, abstract or narrative, recalling a Klimt painting, or a frozen waterfall. Each, too, makes its own contribution to the world of Swarovski, the ultimate expression of Swarovski's universe of crystal creativity.

Collage by Rosemarie Le Gallais

LUNA dressing-table tidy
Collection of designer objects, SS 2002
Darko Mladenovic
Cherry-wood marquetry adorned with a faceted crystal ring

itect

of enchantment

Swarovski crystal is cut crystal. Like a kiss, Swarovski's state-of-the-art precision-cutting techniques awaken the life, light, and beauty that lie quietly waiting within the raw material. Originally developed over 100 years ago by the founder, Daniel Swarovski I, and continually improved and perfected through the years, Swarovski's precision-cutting technology is able to build a complex structure of inter-active facets, planes, and reflections, playing with line, light, and form, and giving the crystal its powerful architectural quality.

The element of cutting and architectural construction gives cut crystal its unique properties, but, operating on another level, it also tells of the company's highly sophisticated and structured search for technical innovation.

NIRVANA ring
SS 1996 collection
Cut crystal

GLACIER ring
"Polychrome" collection, SS 2001
Jet-black cut crystal

Architect *of enchantment* .12

SWAN lamp
Collection of designer objects, SS 2002
Darko Mladenovic
Metallic tube with a block of faceted crystal

KRYSTALLOS fountain pen
Collection of designer objects, SS 2002
Darko Mladenovic in collaboration with
Caran d'Ache
Piece of crystal with long facets, concealed
ink reservoir, silver cap, and rhodium-plated
18-carat solid gold nib
Limited edition

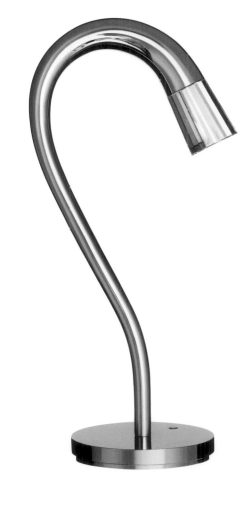

Swarovski's expertise and creativity originated with the invention and construction of machines to cut crystal with unprecedented precision and consistency. Far more than a technical challenge, the whole design esthetic and product development at the core of the company hinges on crystal-cutting, so that cutting technology has evolved as an integral ingredient of Swarovski's identity and visual vocabulary. Crystal-cutting suggests shapes and themes for architecturally inspired objects, jewels for the home, conspiring with jewels and accessories to layer our lives with beauty.

Daniel Swarovski objects follow a tradition, established at the start of the brand, of inviting designers to examine and subvert the roots of the cut-crystal object, and to explore contemporary interpretations of light and form. Today, designer Darko Mladenovic turns his talent to sculptural crystal objects for the home: a bowl, a lamp, a design object to bring beauty into everyday life.

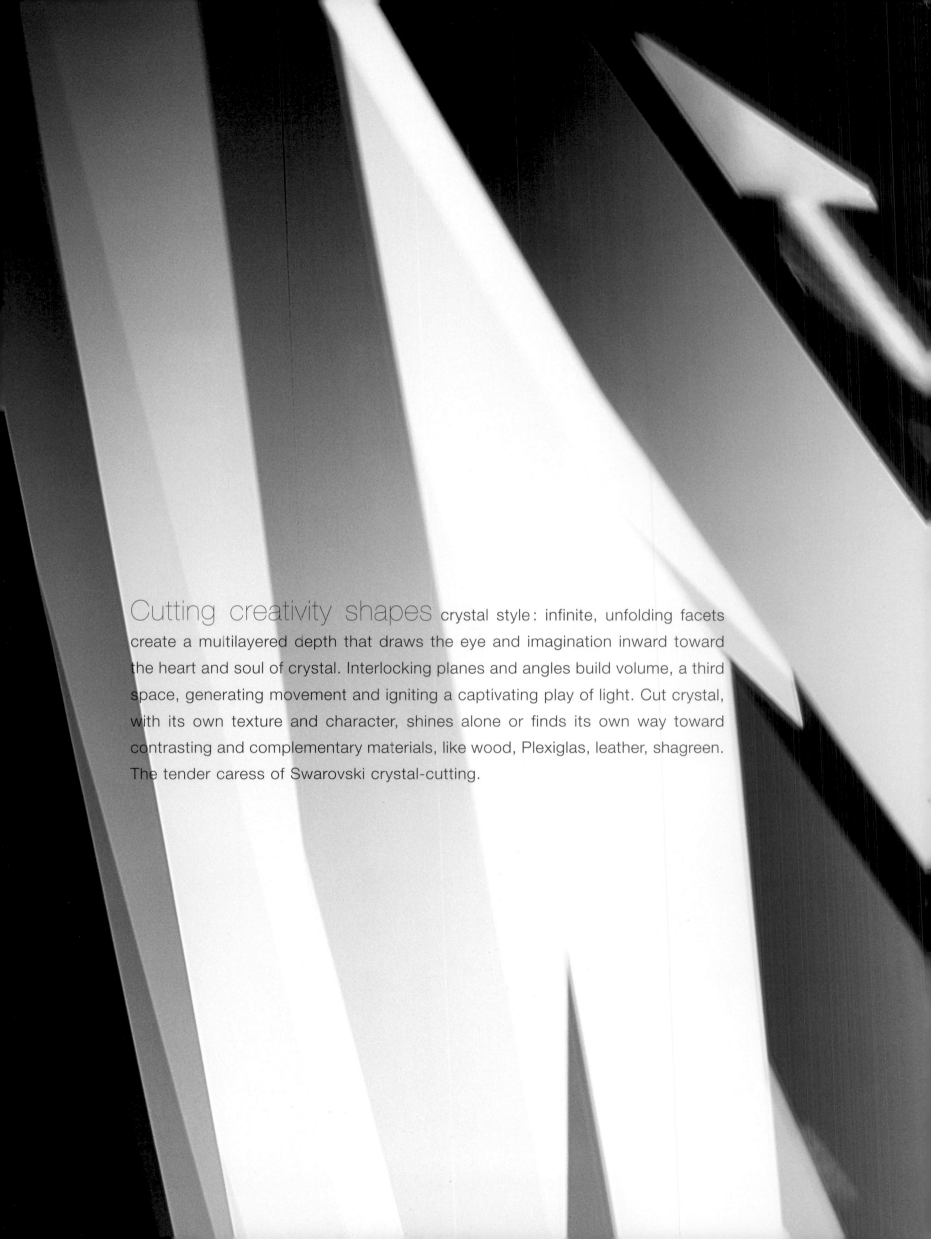

Cutting creativity shapes crystal style: infinite, unfolding facets create a multilayered depth that draws the eye and imagination inward toward the heart and soul of crystal. Interlocking planes and angles build volume, a third space, generating movement and igniting a captivating play of light. Cut crystal, with its own texture and character, shines alone or finds its own way toward contrasting and complementary materials, like wood, Plexiglas, leather, shagreen. The tender caress of Swarovski crystal-cutting.

Detail of RAY art object
Collection of designer objects, SS 2002
Darko Mladenovic
Block of cut crystal
Limited edition

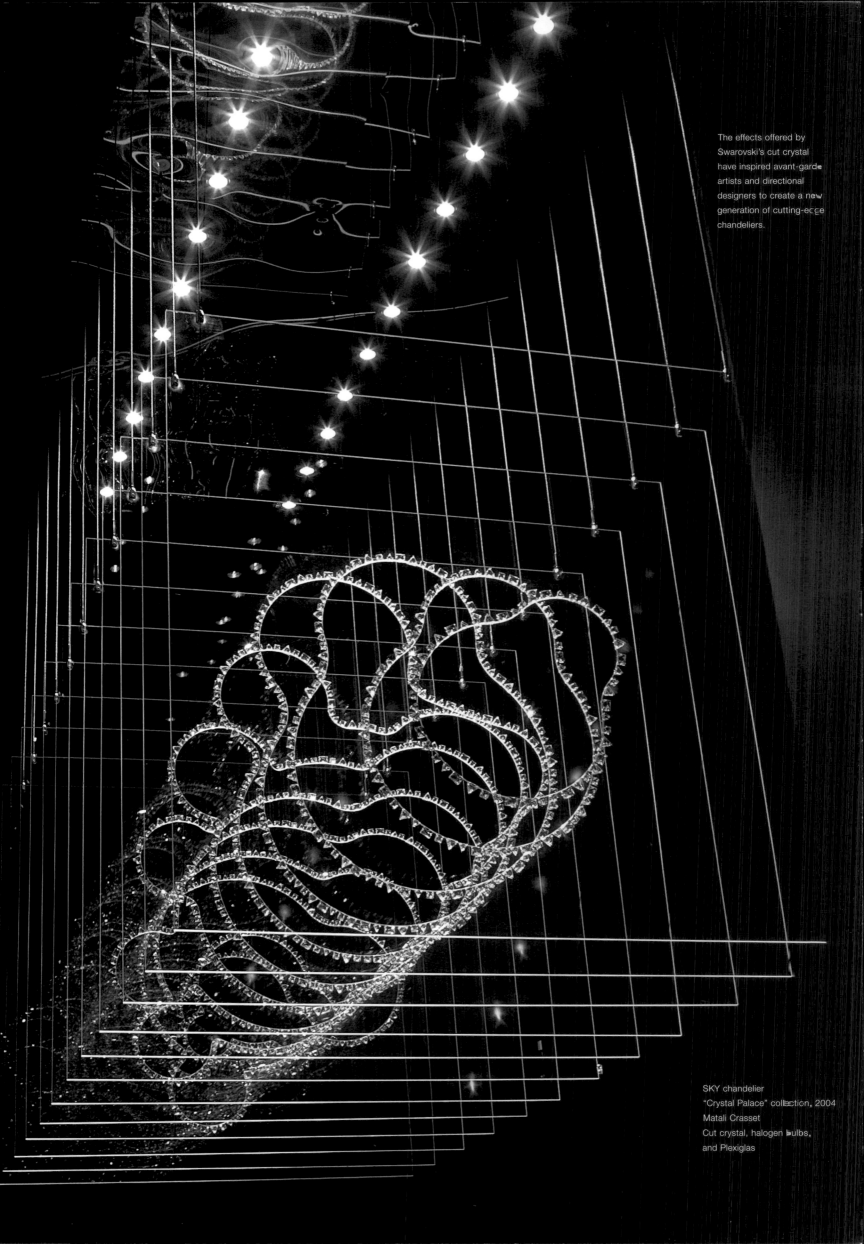

The effects offered by
Swarovski's cut crystal
have inspired avant-garde
artists and directional
designers to create a new
generation of cutting-edge
chandeliers.

SKY chandelier
"Crystal Palace" collection, 2004
Matali Crasset
Cut crystal, halogen bulbs,
and Plexiglas

Sculptures in light. Light is the soul of cut crystal. Prismatic and enigmatic, crystal has a unique way of handling light, sunlight, or candlelight, catching and holding it, as if capturing a moonbeam, and then sending it out again into the world, sliced into shards of color, or shredded into myriad flickering fragments of fire. This scintillating play of light changes with each movement of a crystal stone, chandelier part, or crystal object, like a kaleidoscope, constantly intriguing and fascinating. Beyond the physical, crystal seems to hold and reflect the light of life; light, the universal, primordial symbol of the divine. Working with crystal is like painting with light, drawing with drops, lines and points of shimmering light. Composing with the rhythms and textures of transparency, luminosity, and shadows. Crystal illuminates all things beautiful. It adds a radiance, a sense of wonder, glamor, and celebration to fashion, jewels, treasured objects, and home accessories. Crystal lights up our lives.

OVERNIGHT bag
"Cosmos" collection, FW 2004 / 05
Rabbit fur and buckle paved with crystal

Crystal *intimacy*

Crystal intimacy

Jewelry has an intimate relationship with the body, just as women have a very personal relationship with their jewels, their most powerful expression of individuality. The Daniel Swarovski collection invites women to express themselves, their dreams and desires, through jewelry and accessories, and particularly through crystal, master of moods, capable of reflecting the personality of the wearer. Reveling in its own multifaceted personality, crystal becomes a vehicle for sensuality, moving seductively with the body, like a second skin, and drawing light, and attention, tantalizingly to each movement.

Daniel Swarovski brings crystal closer to the body, giving it a body-conscious softness, a luxuriance of color, cut, translucency, and form, torrents of crystals, tactile textures. At the same time, Daniel Swarovski gives crystal a new depth of emotion, injecting art, beauty, and poetry into everyday life. Creating jewels, accessories, and objects that become part of you, an extension of your personality, intimate crystal for personal pleasure.

NEWTON bag
"Riviera Rock" collection, SS 2004
Lambskin and Crystal Mesh

ONDE necklace
"Cosmos" collection, FW 2004 / 05
Tie-shaped necklace with crystallized
Aurora Borealis twists

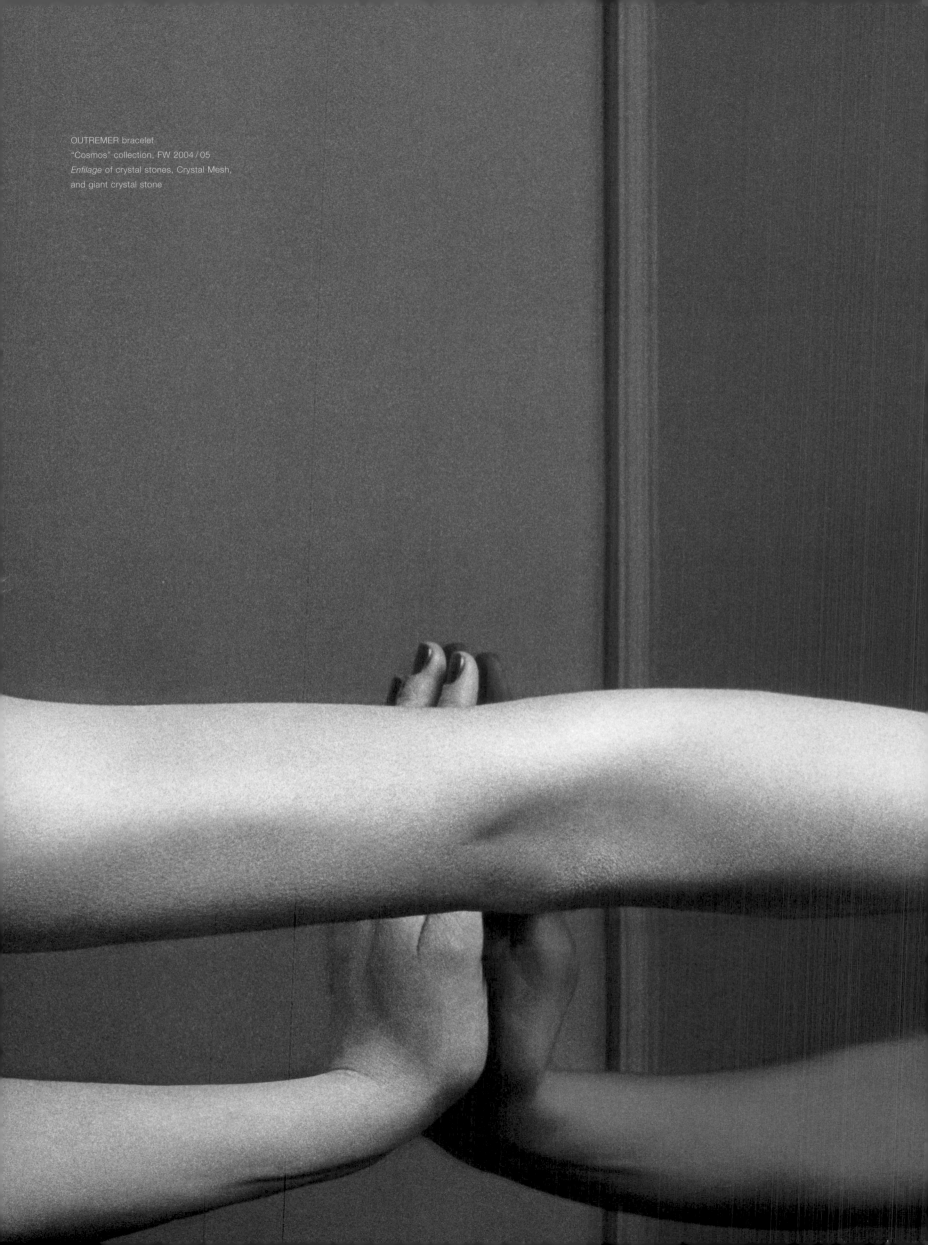

OUTREMER bracelet
"Cosmos" collection, FW 2004 / 05
Enfilage of crystal stones, Crystal Mesh,
and giant crystal stone

INTENSE top
"Sur la route de la soie" collection, FW 2002 / 03
Hematite-crystal Pearl Mesh

The Future through crystal.

Crystal is a material that lives in the moment and looks into the future. Clarity, light, and depth all work together to give crystal an eternal quality: timeless, yet totally in tune with the spirit of each age. Crystal exudes nobility, yet it is also a disseminator of luxury and design excellence. The company's founder, Daniel Swarovski I, saw crystal as a vehicle for bringing artistry and beauty into everyday life, giving a "soul" to objects we wear, use, or keep close to us, bringing pleasure and luxury to the widest possible audience. Crystal invites innovation, both within Swarovski and amongst the international design community. Paying homage to the past whilst generating tomorrow's ideas, Swarovski instigates international design projects in which crystal brings creative visions to life: Crystal Palace challenges the world's leading architects and designers to reinvent the chandelier; Runway Rocks spotlights the art of catwalk jewelry, inviting international designers to create their vision for fashion jewelry of the future. Daniel Swarovski creations have led the way forward, opening up unforeseen possibilities. They show how the extraordinary qualities of crystal, its contrasts and contradictions, its brilliance, sensuality, and emotion, join forces with the most provocative, progressive themes and inspirations, propelling the art of crystal into the future.

Acknowledgments

Our thanks to the designers, stylists, artists, photographers, models, and their associated agencies—
as well as to the many magazines worldwide—who kindly gave their permission to reprint the works
contained in this book.

Special thanks to Rosemarie Le Gallais, Daniel Swarovski's Creative Director,
for her invaluable contribution to the development and design of this book, as well as to Mathilde Janson,
who so generously shared her extensive knowledge of Daniel Swarovski creations.

Credits

All Daniel Swarovski jewels and accessories are designed under the creative direction of Rosemarie Le Gallais.

First published in the United Kingdom in 2005
by Thames & Hudson Ltd, 181A High Holborn,
London WC1V 7QX

www.thamesandhudson.com

© 2005 Swarovski AG

Project realized by The Creative Factory
Creative Direction: Pierre-Yves Chays
Art Direction: Carine Lesor
Text: Vivienne Becker

British Library Cataloguing-in-Publication Data
A catalogue record for this book is available from
the British Library

ISBN-13: 978-0-500-97652-4
ISBN-10: 0-500-97652-X

Typeset in Helvetica Roman 55 (text),
Helvetica Light 45 (captions),
and Didot LH Roman (headings)
Jacket: GardaMatt 200 gsm
Inside pages: GardaMatt 170 gsm
Printed and bound in Italy by Conti Tipocolor